Benjamin Franklin

A Life of Science and Service

Steven Jay Griffel

Boston, Massachusetts
Chandler, Arizona
Glenview, Illinois
Upper Saddle River, New Jersey

Illustrations
2, 3, 4, 7, 8 Nathan Trewartha.

Photographs
Every effort has been made to secure permission and provide appropriate credit for photographic material. The publisher deeply regrets any omission and pledges to correct errors called to its attention in subsequent editions.

Unless otherwise acknowledged, all photographs are the property of Pearson Education, Inc.

Photo locators denoted as follows: Top (T), Center (C), Bottom (B), Left (L), Right (R), Background (Bkgd)

Opener: Kim Sayer/©DK Images; 1 Kim Sayer/©DK Images; 6 Library of Congress; 11 Library of Congress; 12 National Archives; 13 Library of Congress.

ISBN-13: 978-0-328-67694-1
ISBN-10: 0-328-67694-2

7 V0FL 16 15 14 13

Who Was Benjamin Franklin?

When Ben Franklin signed the Declaration of Independence, he was already 70 years old. He was the oldest American to sign the Declaration. He was also, perhaps, the most famous American of his time. In many ways, he was better known than Paul Revere, George Washington, or Thomas Jefferson.

By 1776, Franklin's many accomplishments had earned him worldwide fame. You might even say that Franklin was a world celebrity. All across America and Europe, people knew Ben Franklin's work. They knew him as an inventor, scientist, writer, and **diplomat**, or official representative of the government overseas.

Franklin's life became one of the first American success stories. Born into a poor family, he was one of 17 children. Through hard work, Franklin built his fame—and his fortune. Today, Franklin still represents the American "can-do" spirit. As Americans of the twenty-first century, we can learn a great deal from his life.

Franklin's Childhood

Many leaders of the American Revolution, such as George Washington and Thomas Jefferson, came from wealthy families, but not Ben Franklin. Born in Boston on January 17, 1706, Franklin was the youngest son in his family. Like most boys of the time, Franklin expected to become an **apprentice**. His brothers had been apprentices, sent off from home at a young age to learn a trade, such as candle-making or printing.

In exchange for learning a trade, apprentices had to work for a master for ten or more years. Yet, for most colonial boys, an apprenticeship seemed like a good deal. After all, they could learn valuable skills and then, once free to go out on their own, they could earn a decent living. One of Franklin's brother's, James, had been a printer's apprentice. Now, James owned his own print shop.

During Franklin's time, apprentices often worked in trades such as these:

Blacksmith maker of horseshoes, nails, and tools

Shoemaker maker of shoes, a trade practiced in America since 1610

Carpenter and Joiner builders who use wood

Silversmith maker of silverware and other household items

Cooper maker of casks and barrels

Wheelwright maker of wheels for wagons and carts

Becoming an Apprentice

Franklin didn't become an apprentice at first. Instead, he was sent to school because his family hoped that Franklin would become a minister. However, they had to pay for Franklin's school, and they could not afford it. After just two years, Franklin's father took him out of school. Franklin, now ten, became his father's apprentice. Franklin's father planned to teach him to be a soap-maker and candle-maker. Franklin, however, had other plans.

Franklin knew that his schooling was over, but he was determined to get a good education. He read every book he could find. Franklin often begged other apprentices to let him borrow books from their masters. Sometimes, he had to promise to read a book in one day to make sure the book could be returned before the master missed it. By the time Franklin was 12, his father knew that his son was a skilled reader—and a very unhappy candle-maker. As a result, Franklin's father sent him to be an apprentice in his brother James's print shop.

Soon after Franklin started apprenticing at the print shop, James knew that his youngest brother would make a great printer. Franklin was a skilled reader, a good writer, and a hard worker, all qualities that early American printers needed in their workers. During the colonial era, finding workers with good reading and writing skills was difficult, so James signed his young brother to a long apprenticeship. Franklin was now obligated to work for James for nine years.

Franklin in Philadelphia

While working as a printer's apprentice, Franklin began to develop his own writing style. When he was only 16, he wrote a series of humorous letters. In secret, he sent the letters to his brother, signing them "Mrs. Silence Dogood." His brother printed the letters in the newspaper, which James had just recently started. Although the letters amused many people, Franklin's brother was not one of them.

Here is an excerpt from Franklin's third "Silence Dogood" letter, published on April 30, 1722. Note that young Franklin already felt a duty to help his fellow citizens.

It is undoubtedly the Duty of all Persons to serve the Country they live in....I now take up a Resolution, to do for the future all that lies in my Way for the Service of my Countrymen.

Franklin and his brother argued about the letters and many other things. James, as the master, even hit Franklin, something that many other masters also did to their apprentices. After a while, Franklin wanted to be free of his brother and escape from the print shop. Legally, however, Franklin was bound to finish out his long term of apprenticeship. If he stayed in Boston, Franklin knew he would most likely be forced to keep working for his brother. So, he decided to go to Philadelphia, which was growing rapidly. Franklin felt that he had a better chance to make something of himself there. In 1723, at age 17, Franklin secretly left on a ship out of Boston with little more than the clothes he wore.

Business Owner

When Franklin arrived in Philadelphia, he did not know anyone and he only had enough money to buy some rolls. Fortunately, he soon found work as a printer and set about making a good impression on the people of Philadelphia. Just a few years later, Franklin was ready to strike out on his own. With the help of friends, he started his own print shop business. He was only 22 years old.

Franklin worked hard at his printing business. To expand his sales, he decided to publish an almanac. At the time, these inexpensive books were very popular. They were easy to read and contained information that people found both entertaining and educational. Franklin called his almanac *Poor Richard's Almanack*. It contained funny stories, jokes, and **proverbs**, or wise sayings, that Franklin mostly wrote. It also had a calendar and weather forecasts.

Franklin's almanac became the most popular almanac in colonial America. Thanks in large part to its success, Franklin became wealthy and well known all over the colonies. By this time, he was 42 years old, a husband, a father, and a well-known businessperson. Franklin was now ready to try something new.

Poor Richard, 1733.
AN
Almanack
For the Year of Chriſt
1733,
Being the Firſt after LEAP YEAR:

And makes ſince the Creation	Years
By the Account of the Eastern *Greeks*	7241
By the Latin Church, when ☉ ent. ♈	6932
By the Computation of *W. W.*	5742
By the *Roman* Chronology	5682
By the *Jewish* Rabbies	5494

Wherein is contained
The Lunations, Eclipſes, Judgment of the Weather, Spring Tides, Planets Motions & mutual Aſpects, Sun and Moon's Riſing and Setting, Length of Days, Time of High Water, Fairs, Courts, and obſervable Days.
Fitted to the Latitude of Forty Degrees, and a Meridian of Five Hours Weſt from *London*, but may without ſenſible Error, ſerve all the adjacent Places, even from *Newfoundland* to *South-Carolina*.
By *RICHARD SAUNDERS*, Philom.
PHILADELPHIA:
Printed and ſold by *B. FRANKLIN*, at the New Printing-Office near the Market.

Franklin published his *Almanack* under the name Richard Saunders. Franklin often used made-up names for his publications.

Community Leader

Unlike today, colonial America did not have the town and city services and **institutions**, or established organizations, that we often take for granted. Thus, Franklin decided to put his skills and wealth to work in service to his community. Franklin felt it was his duty as a citizen to help his community. No **civic** duty was too large or too small for him. For example, Philadelphia had many muddy and dark streets. Franklin worked to get the city's streets paved and better lit. He also helped form Philadelphia's first fire-fighting company.

Franklin remembered how important reading had been in his childhood. Books, however, were still hard to come by in colonial times. To help solve this problem, Franklin set up America's first circulating library. He also raised money for the first hospital in America. Franklin even helped create the postal system we use today. Not only did Franklin's post offices make a profit, they also helped link the colonies together.

From Poor Richard's Proverbs:

- A penny saved is a penny earned.
- An ounce of prevention is worth a pound of cure.
- Eat to live, and not live to eat.
- Early to bed and early to rise, makes a man healthy, wealthy, and wise.
- The worst wheel of a cart makes the most noise.
- Fish and visitors stink after three days.
- Well done is better than well said.
- The sleeping Fox catches no poultry. Up! Up!

Inventor and Scientist

Franklin also worked hard to come up with practical solutions to everyday problems. In his time, houses were poorly heated. Most of the heat came from fireplaces—and it went right out the chimney. People had to burn a lot of wood, yet they still couldn't keep warm.

To help solve this problem, Franklin designed a new stove. His stove needed less wood and it created more heat. Franklin's design enabled more of the stove's heat to warm a room, rather than be wasted. Franklin designed his stoves so they did not cost a lot of money. That way, more people could afford them.

Franklin invented many new products and devices. He invented bifocals, a new type of eyeglasses. Franklin also invented the odometer, a device that measures how far a vehicle travels. As postmaster, Franklin used his odometer to determine how far postal wagons traveled. He wanted to determine which routes were the shortest to take for delivering the mail.

Franklin enjoyed reading the latest books about science and conducting his own experiments. Franklin's most famous experiment involved electricity. Franklin thought that lightning was a form of electricity. With the help of his adult son William, Franklin set out to prove his idea in 1752.

The way the story is told, the two men flew a kite during a thunderstorm. A large key was tied to the end of the kite string. When the lightning hit the kite, electricity traveled down the string. When it reached the key, Franklin saw an electric spark. This proved his **theory**, or idea, that lightning was indeed electricity. Most scientists think that Franklin performed the experiment in a much safer way than it has been told. If Franklin had done the experiment as described, he probably would have been killed.

Ever the practical person, Franklin followed up his discovery by inventing the lightning rod. These metal rods were placed on buildings to protect them from lightning, a major cause of house fires back then. Franklin's inventions made him more money, and they made him even more famous.

The story about the kite has been told and illustrated many times. The artist of this drawing thought incorrectly that Franklin's son was still a boy.

Public Servant

Despite the success of his inventions, Franklin considered public service his most important civic duty. For years, he had worked to improve life in Philadelphia. At age 50, Franklin decided to take a more active role in colonial politics. Franklin was well suited for this work. He was as practical and skilled in politics as he was in inventing.

Stopping the Stamp Act

In 1764, Franklin agreed to go to Great Britain to represent the Pennsylvania colony. There, his political skills were put to the test on behalf of all the colonies. Parliament had passed the Stamp Act. This law required the colonists to buy special stamps for newspapers, court papers, and other documents. In effect, the Stamp Act raised taxes on the colonists.

Members of Parliament and King George III expected the colonists to obey all British laws. However, they refused to let the colonists elect representatives to serve in Parliament. Many colonists grew angry at how they were being ruled by the British. They viewed the Stamp Act and their lack of representation in the British government as very unfair.

Franklin hoped he could reach a solution with the British. Because of Franklin's accomplishments, the British greatly respected him. Franklin, however, realized that the British looked down at most Americans. Often, the British used the word *American* as an insulting term. Franklin knew he would have a hard time convincing Parliament to repeal the Stamp Act.

For four hours, Franklin presented his arguments to Parliament. He answered many questions, some of which were insulting to Americans. Franklin kept calm and did not show his anger. In the end, Parliament agreed with Franklin and repealed the Stamp Act. With this success, Franklin became the leading voice for the Americans in Britain.

For the next several years, Franklin spent much of his time in Britain. He tried to maintain good relations between Britain and its American colonies. Franklin's **mission**, or goal, however, grew more difficult. Parliament continued to pass laws that angered the colonists, who in turn continued to protest against British rule. One of the more hated acts that Parliament passed was the Tea Act, in 1773. Colonists in Boston responded to the act by disguising themselves. Then, they took over three tea ships and dumped hundreds of boxes of tea into Boston Harbor.

Colonists protested the Stamp Act. In this picture, colonists burn Stamp Act papers in Boston.

Franklin and the Fight for American Independence

Parliament passed new laws to punish the colonies for their protests, especially for the Boston Tea Party. Many colonists lost hope of ever being treated fairly by the British. In 1774, colonists sent representatives to a special meeting, the First Continental Congress. They voted to halt all trade with Britain and to start training troops. Naturally, Parliament grew even more furious.

Back in Britain, Franklin again urged Parliament to find a peaceful solution. This time, Parliament refused to listen to him. Franklin knew in his heart that war was coming. He returned home to America.

By the time Franklin arrived back home in the late spring of 1775, the battles of Lexington and Concord had been fought. Franklin was nearly seventy years old now, but he decided to do all he could to ensure American independence. Elected as a **delegate**, or representative, from Pennsylvania to the Second Continental Congress, he helped draft the Declaration of Independence.

If the Revolution failed, everyone who signed the Declaration of Independence could have been put to death. Franklin's signature showed how much he was willing to risk for his country. Can you find his signature?

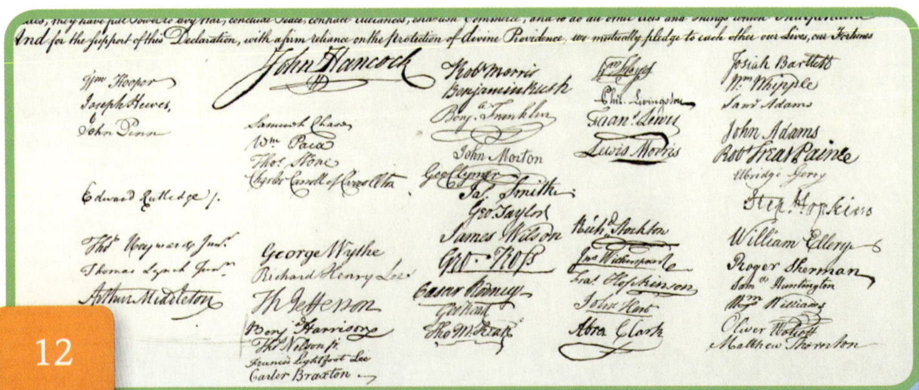
And for the support of this Declaration, with a firm reliance on the protection of divine Providence, we mutually pledge to each other our Lives, our Fortunes

Even in fancy French palaces, Franklin dressed in simple clothing. To the French, he was an American hero. His popularity helped Franklin convince the French king to help the American cause.

American Diplomat in France

By late 1776, the Americans were struggling to hold off the British. They lacked money for supplies and weapons. To win the war, the Americans knew they needed an ally. Knowing that Franklin was such a convincing speaker, Congress sent Franklin to France. His job was to persuade French King Louis XVI to give the Americans military and financial aid.

When Franklin arrived in France, he was already well known there. Franklin enjoyed the many parties given in his honor. He befriended many important people in France. Then, he worked with his new friends to win over the French king. By helping the Americans, Franklin told the king, the French could stop the British from expanding their empire.

Franklin served in France for about eight years. During this time, he persuaded French officials to keep money and supplies flowing to America. When the fighting stopped, Franklin helped complete the formal **treaty**, or official agreement, that ended the war. By this time, he was nearly eighty and ready to return home for good.

While Franklin was in France, the American Revolution had been fought and won. Though he had not fired one shot in defense of his country, Franklin had sacrificed a great deal. For years, he had lived overseas, far from most of his family and friends. Without his efforts, America might not have had the resources it needed to defeat the British.

On the long voyage home, most men of his age and status would have relaxed, but not Franklin. He kept busy by designing a new stove and planning ways to improve sailing ships. When he arrived in Philadelphia on September 14, 1785, he was greeted as a national hero.

Soon after arriving, Franklin went right back to work. He was chosen to help draft a new national constitution. Franklin joined 54 delegates from around the country to write a new plan, the United States Constitution. His service at the meeting—called the Constitutional Convention—would be his last official public duty.

A Timeline of Franklin's Life

1706
Ben Franklin is born in Boston.

1700 **1710** **1720** **1730** **1740**

1723
Franklin goes to Philadelphia.

During his final years, Franklin kept working on new inventions. He also wrote newspaper articles and letters to many friends and political leaders. In 1790, only months before his death, Franklin sent a letter to the United States government asking that slavery be ended. Even until the very end of his life, Benjamin Franklin did all he could in service for his country. From humble beginnings, Franklin rose to become one of the great American leaders of all time.

Franklin's fame lives on today. We are reminded of Franklin's contributions to America every day. Across the United States, we can see the bridges, highways, and schools named in his honor. Stamps, statues, and the $100 bill show us his famous face. Through his example, Franklin has taught generations of Americans to work hard and to do their civic duty. His life's story still serves to inspire all of us.

You can see this statue in Philadelphia, at the Benjamin Franklin National Memorial.

1765 Stamp Act is passed.

1766 Stamp Act is repealed.

1776 Declaration of Independence is signed.

1776 Franklin goes to France.

1785 Franklin returns to America.

1787 The U.S. Constitution is signed.

1790 Franklin dies.

1760 1770 1780 1790 1790

Glossary

apprentice a young person who agreed to work for someone for a set period of time in exchange for learning a trade or skill

civic related to being a citizen

delegate someone who represents others, such as an elected representative in government

diplomat person who officially represents the government in its dealings with foreign governments

institution an established organization that performs a public service, such as a hospital or a college

mission a goal or assignment

proverb a wise saying

theory a scientific statement that explains natural events, such as lightning or why Earth revolves around the sun

treaty an agreement between countries or groups